I0143428

My
Doo-Dah
Days

Copyright 2012, Alfred Pollock

All rights reserved. Printed in the U.S.A.

No part of this publication may be reproduced or transmitted in
any form or by any means, electronic or mechanical, including
photocopy, recording or any information storage and retrieval
system now known or to be invented, without permission in
writing from the publisher, except by a reviewer who wishes
to quote brief passages in connection with a review written for
inclusion in a magazine, newspaper or broadcast.

Published in the United States by
Beckham Publications Group, Inc.
P.O. Box 4066, Silver Spring, MD 20914

ISBN: 978-0-9848243-7-3

My Doo-Dah Days

Fifty Adventurous Years as a Horse Trainer and Owner

Alfred Pollock

THE Beckham
PUBLICATIONS GROUP, INC.

Silver Spring

Contents

Introduction

May 16, 1952, my thirteenth birthday, was a glorious day. I arrived breathless at Belmont Racetrack at 12:45, which gave me a half hour until post time. Since I rarely had more than ten dollars after admission, financial partnerships were a necessity in order to get down for every race. My own consortium consisted of Chalky Jack, a WWII veteran; Chico, a retired pilot; Whitey (I know he did something), and yours truly. We would buy shares of two dollar tickets at 50 cents each if we liked the same horse. However, if there was a difference of opinion, we were either on our own or we had to form new temporary partnerships. No problem on this day, though. We all liked Hambone in the first.

The announcer said, "It is now post time," and, like everyone else, I stood up on my seat. I raised my Roy Rogers binoculars and lit a cigarette. This day, aside from its being my birthday, was no different from any other school day.

I had gotten in touch with my love of horses when I was eight years old. I was taken to the movies to see *The Story of Seabiscuit* (1949 version). Well, it was like the first time Mozart saw a piano. After that, I sat through it a second time. I would have stayed for a third, but I was dragged out, kicking and screaming.

After that, the only movies that interested me were racing flicks. There was *Kentucky* with Walter Brennan and Loretta Young, *Kentucky Blue Grass* with Billy Williams, *The Story of Black Gold* with Adolph Menjou, *The Killing* with Sterling

Hayden, and, of course, the greatest of them all: *A Day at the Races* with the Marx Brothers. When there were no racing movies around, I'd look for Westerns, just to see the horses. The only horses I had seen up close had policemen on their backs who, although they wouldn't let me ride, did allow me to pet their horses' noses.

Ultimately, as a result of my tenacity and continuous nagging, my mother capitulated and took me to The Manhattan Riding Academy on West 66th Street. On your first visit, you had to ride around a ring so the owner could see if you could ride safely or not. As I was about to mount Mickey, the owner asked if I had ridden much before.

I replied, "I've been riding all my life."

Once I was on the horse, he had no reason to doubt me. It came so naturally, it was easier than walking. I don't know where it came from but, if you believe in nature over nurture, my maternal grandfather was a cavalry officer. My father's father, on the other hand, was a rabbi who would probably have been quite upset when I was thrown out of Hebrew School.

I spent the better part of my high school years in places named Belmont, Jamaica, Aqueduct, Bowie, Pimlico and Lincoln Downs. Since there was no winter racing in the East in those days I went to school. If I was in school in the spring or the fall I was broke. For me, school was a punishment for picking losers.

1

School Days

They say that high school prepares you for college, but Commerce High School on the Upper West Side in New York City was, more than anything else, a preparation for Rikers Island, the city's main jail complex. On day one, the freshman class was informed that, if we were expelled, the next stop was either reform school or the Army. We were reminded who we were.

Nonetheless, when this informative assembly concluded, I managed to angle out of a side door and easily make it to Belmont for the first race. In order to accomplish this on a daily basis, meticulous planning was necessary. On an average weekday, I'd arrive at school with the daily *Racing Form* concealed in *The New York Times*, a pack of Camels (25 cents), my binoculars in a brown paper bag that resembled lunch, and my betting money in my right front pants pocket—as opposed to my eating money, which was in my left pocket.

My betting money came from selling Christmas cards in the fall in response to an ad in my comic books which said, "Make extra money in your spare time!" As any door-to-door salesman will tell you, there's a lot of resistance out there. Mine was in the form of religious objections. People would get rid of me by saying "Oh, we're Jewish" (even if they weren't), "we don't send Christmas cards."

While I wasn't about to talk them out of their religion, I could change my samples. I pulled out all the cards that mentioned

Christmas and replaced them with cards showing winter scenes with no mention of Christmas, and only a message of season's greetings or holiday wishes.

Now, when I was dismissed with the religious objection, I would say "I'm Jewish also, and I have just what you're looking for. These are the cards that my parents send over the holidays." What could they say now? They were trapped. I had turned their no into a "yes." I guess I can thank Currier and Ives for staking my first bankroll.

So here I am, sitting in civics class, just waiting. It was crucial that I hit the street no later than 11 a.m. I can't overstate the precision involved to ensure that I wouldn't miss the first race. Intricate maneuvers had to be employed simply to get out of the building. Bear in mind, I'm not dealing here with 11th grade hall monitors looking for extra credit. At Commerce High School, the doors were monitored by well-armed, uniformed New York City Police.

There was a three minute interval between classes when the doors were left unattended because of the changing of the guards. When the bell rang to end third period, I was poised to sprint down the stairs and out the door faster than my future horses ever did. I can't describe the blast of freedom when I hit 66th Street. Only Nelson Mandela could fully appreciate the exhilaration of my release after two-and-a-half hours of hellish boredom. Now, with the worst over, I am still looking at three trains and a bus before I get to the track in Elmont. This gave me plenty of time to do my homework.

By this I mean, of course, studying the day's entries. I'd arrive at Belmont in Long Island at around 12:45, and follow the scent of the horses straight to the paddock. Even though I had been going to the track regularly for five years, it was still unbearably exciting the moment I walked in. The void I experienced almost everywhere else was then filled.

While the other kids were studying for their SATs and fretting about their futures, I was comfortable in the knowledge that this is where I would spend the rest of my life. All I had to figure out was how.

Somehow I managed to convince myself that in spite of a 5'10" 165 pound frame, I could shrink myself enough to be a jockey. I dieted rigorously. That lasted for about six weeks until I couldn't stand being dizzy anymore. That's when I made up my mind that I would be a trainer. But my career path would not be without some bumps in the road. The next few years were uneventful as I continued to spend my spring and fall at the track as much as I could while maintaining my abbreviated school schedule.

In June of 1957, I graduated from high school. No sooner was the diploma in my hand, than I stuffed it into *The New York Times* with my *Racing Form* and headed to Belmont to celebrate.

When I ran into the guys, Chico asked, "Why so formal?" I realized I still had my tie on, and told him that somehow I just graduated from high school. "You got a job lined up?"

I told him that I would be looking for something maybe just for the summer. That's when I finally found out what Whitey did. It seems he was personnel manager for Anthony "Fat Tony" Salerno, a well-known East Harlem entrepreneur who happened to have some openings in his organization. He explained to me that they needed someone who knew gambling and could "keep their mouth shut." I would be taking bets on numbers, sports and horses. I hesitated, but my mind was made up for me when he added, "You'll start at five bucks an hour and you have to work Saturday and Sunday."

I tried to hide my excitement. Five bucks an hour? In 1957, the minimum wage was less than a dollar an hour. Although I had been planning to work on the backstretch, this was an opportunity to get everything I wanted. Between this and my Christmas cards, I could save enough money to get a car and a racehorse. That's all I wanted.

By 1961, between the Christmas cards, my salary, and a few lucky photos, I had accumulated enough money for a new car and a racehorse. I was a little concerned that my employers might be less than gracious regarding my resignation, but my fears were for naught. The last thing they said, was "Good luck kid, let us know when you have a winner."

And so, clueless but optimistic, I headed South.

2

Equine Studies 101

My backstretch training was done in Tampa, Florida with a female trainer named Iva Mae Parrish. I chose to learn from her because in 1962 a female horse trainer was like a Jewish coal miner . . . . rare! So, I figured she had to be good, and I was right. That's when my Doo Dah days began.

The Doo Dah begins about 5:00 a.m., which means you had to set your clock radio for 4:30. To make sure I would get up, I would have it set to the Jacksonville egg market prices which, if you didn't own any eggs, was a guarantee to get you up to turn it off. Once you're up and you know your horses are expecting you with their breakfast, there's no going back.

It's rarely more than a ten minute drive to the track at that hour since the only traffic you hit is at the stable gate. When you arrive at your barn the first thing you do is empty and refill the horses' water buckets, then give them one measure (usually a coffee can.) of oats to shut them up, then it's off to feed yourself at a nearby diner or the track kitchen.

For most horse-people, early breakfast consists of black coffee, several cigarettes, and the day's *Racing Form*. The health-conscious ones included sugar doughnuts in their daily regimen. Or, as Tommy Sisum used to say, "Gimme one of them thar squeegee rolls." When the sky begins to look like old dimes, the work day begins. Work times varied little from track to track, generally starting at 5:30 a.m.—the exception being

Gulfstream where, because of the Florida heat, we began at 3:30 and finished before 8:30. That's when the sun would rise over the condominiums, making it too hot to train.

Me and the other boondockers, or gypsies (as one—and two-horse stables were known) generally started our day trying to make extra money helping the larger stable "git done." This was done by walking "hots" (horses need to be walked at least a half an hour after exercising on the track) or, like me, ponying horses (an exercise faster than a trot, slower than a gallop). The racehorse is bareback with only his halter on. A shank (or leash-like device) is connected within the halter, which gives the outrider some control.

Freelance pony boys got $2.00 for one mile in the mornings, $5.00 for taking a racehorse to the post in the afternoon, and occasionally an extra $10.00 if we brought a winner to the post. Those were the going rates, but sometimes it was as easy to get paid as finding Geronimo's autograph, especially on or near getaway day (end of meeting) when everyone is looking for shipping money North, or in my case, South to Gulfstream in North Miami.

3

Culture Shock

The drive from Sunshine Park in Oldsmar, Florida, only takes about five hours, while adapting to the new culture could take five weeks. It was like going from *Hee Haw* to *Sixty Minutes*.

On the Size of the Purses

Sunshine Park . . . . "We're runnin' for ham sandwiches."
Gulf Stream . . . "The purses have increased to just north of bupkis"

On Coffee Breaks

Sunshine Park . . . Pick-up trucks adorned with Confederate flags, stickers, and license plates roamed the stable area, selling coffee and doughnuts.

Gulfstream . . . At six a.m. the smell of fresh baked rugelach wafting in from Pumpernicks could cause a stampede across Hallandale Beach Boulevard if the wind were blowing northwest.

On Paddock Talk

Sunshine Park . . ."How's your horse feeling?"
Response: "Gittin Chesty"

Gulfstream . . . "How's your horse feeling?"
Response: "I don't know, I haven't felt him."

On Entertainment in the Workplace

Sunshine Park . . . Every shed row (barn) has at least one radio on during training hours. Ninety-nine percent of the time it is tuned to a country Western station. I must have heard, "You can't Have Your Kate and Edith Too" ten thousand times.

Gulfstream . . . Usually a news station that gives stock market quotes mixed occasionally with an old goldies' station that featured Lawrence Welk.

On Spousal Relationships

Sunshine Park . . . . "How's the wife?"
Response: "Rank and common."
Gulfstream . . . "How's the wife?"
Response: "I haven't inquired . . . . I don't want to interrupt her."

On Cocktail Hour

Sunshine Park . . .
Time: 9:30 a.m. upon completion of morning work

Place: Most any tack room

Beverage list: white lightning, honey hush or hot Lucy and on special occasions, muscatel.

Conversation: Referring to a recent acquaintance, "Her ass is at least two axe handles." And, on a more serious note, tomorrow's entries.

Gulfstream . . .

Time:	6 p.m. after a quick swim following the last race.
Place:	The Diplomat Lounge
Beverage List:	Very Dry martinis, Perrier with lemon, and Shirley Temples.
Conversation:	"Who's playing at the Fountainbleau? And, on a more serious note, tomorrow's entries.

4

My Summer With Iva Mae, Hasten Home, and The Ku Klux Klan

About ninety miles northeast of Tampa there's a town called Umatilla, that to me resembled a rest area for the Confederate Army. Everybody had a gun because guns were as easy to buy as toothpaste, and frankly, a much bigger seller. Iva Mae had a small farm there and invited me for the summer of '63 to continue my equine education. The only prerequisite was that her barnyard shovel fit my hand . . . it did.

Umatilla Days

Each day after I finished my chores, consisting mainly of manure removal for the 10 horses that she boarded, Iva took the time to teach me. The model she used was Hasten Home, the yearling she bought for 50 cents just minutes before he was to have been euthanized.

Frankly, at first glance, you would think she had grossly overpaid. Starting from the ground up; his ankles didn't match—the left being higher than the right (a birth defect)—and his knees were so weak that they couldn't support the weight of a large dog. Now we come to the main problem—the left shoulder. Because of a deformity in the withers, his left leg moved at a ninety degree angle from the rest of his body. In short, he had more problems than Al Capone at a tax audit. That said, he was perfect to learn from. Iva would show me one of her sound boarders and compare them to Hasten Home.

Every day, Hasten Home and I would go to a lake near her farm. Iva Mae would get into her rowboat and I would lead Hasten home into the water. "Make him swim, Al!" Iva Mae would shout from the boat, and I would pull him into the deep water. That seemed to be the therapy he needed. Since horses are natural swimmers, getting him into water was never a problem. As his condition improved, however, getting him out was another story. He was having too much fun. It wasn't long until Iva Mae said, "Well, Al, I think it's time to take him out on the track."

Sunday mornings in Umatilla were quiet, and every Sunday while the streets were still yawning, Iva Mae would go to church. On a couple of occasions she invited me to join her. Each time I respectfully declined. Finally, because it seemed so important to her, I accompanied her one Sunday to the First Baptist Church of Umatilla. "What religion are you, Al?" she asked me on the way. When I told her I was Jewish, she mustered up the appropriate nonchalance and assured me, "That's nice."

Umatilla Government

The sheriff's office jail and courthouse are located just off Main Street. The facility also housed the headquarters of the local Ku Klux Klan. This arrangement made it convenient for the sheriff, deputy sheriff, and judge who presided over the affairs of all four agencies.

Umatilla Nightlife

Umatilla nightlife started around midnight in the summer. If it was cool enough (70 degrees or so) we could take out the horses that couldn't tolerate the 110 degree heat during the day. If not, there were always warm weather activities to fall back on. I will never forget one particular night in July when it was cool enough to ride My riding companions were gentlemen named Buckshot, Muskie (so named for his legendary capacity for Muscatel), Ditters, and Everett—all armed to the teeth and drunk.

That night, as we proceeded single file into the woods, I thought I would add a little levity to the moment. I rode up to the head of the line, dropped my reins and raised my arms as if to surrender. I then turned to Muskie and said, "Do you know what this is?"

He replied, "W-o-ooot? (What)?

I replied, "The Confederate cavalry on maneuvers,"

Surprisingly, umbrage was taken by all. "Let's git the Yank," were the last words I waited around to hear, before my bare feet pounded on my Appaloosa's ribs in an urgent message to head for the exits. We sped off, and it was fun, until I heard the gunshots deliberately fired over my head but low enough to break the overhead branches. This sent my horse into a frantic gallop while I, bareback and shoeless, draped my arms around his neck, holding on for dear life. There was nothing I learned growing up on West End Avenue in New York City that would prepare me for this moment. Somehow, by following our own trail of crushed palmetto plants and aided by a full summer moon, I made it back uninjured. I went for a swim, and as dawn approached, a barnyard shovel was back in my hand.

While Yankee chasing was always entertaining because it was conducted on horseback, other social arrangements had to be made on hot nights. Umatilla's second favorite pastime, possum hunting, was conducted on foot, making it the warm weather favorite.

On one hot night, my girlfriend Sandy suggested that I accompany her and my newly acquired equestrian companions on a hunt. My first instinct was to decline the invitation. But there was a problem; I didn't ever want to upset Sandy, who seemed to have great influence over these men. Some of them, I gathered, were vaguely related to her, although I was never sure which ones or how. I was pretty sure, however, that my survival rested on her attachment to me.

One day I had overheard her tell Ditters, "I like h-am," ("I like him") which I interpreted to mean, "Don't kill him." Between her and Iva Mac, whose stake in my future was continued free labor, I enjoyed some degree of comfort in these foreign environs.

On that basis, I replied to Sandy's invitation by assuring her, "I wouldn't amiss it!" That wasn't hard, but I shuddered to think how I would react if there was an offer of twice-baked possum in my future.

So there we are, looking for possums in the forest. After only a few minutes, I was starting to regret the fact that I declined the offer of a rifle. What was I thinking? How do I really know that this isn't a setup to kill me after all? They'd never find me here. They could say it was a hunting accident if anyone even cared to ask. What if Sandy called off her protection? Maybe she heard me telling redneck jokes in my sleep. Then I heard guns go off; that's when I learned that possums really *do* play possum. More importantly, that's when I realized, they weren't aiming at me! This continued until around three in the morning, when we all headed back and went for a swim. I had lived to see another Umatilla sunrise with Iva Mae's shovel back in my hand!

That winter in Tampa, two monumental events occurred on the American turf: Hasten Home won his first of 39 races, coming from last in the stretch, and I passed my trainer's test. I found that out when I heard the announcement over the PA system, "Will trainer A.W. Pollock please report to the steward's office." I got there so fast, I arrived while the message was being repeated, and accepted congratulations on the fact that I got a 99% mark on the written test.

As I walked back to the grandstand, I noticed my world had changed. I was a trainer. Oh doo dah day!

Now, all I needed was a racehorse.

Iva Mae's barn in Tampa

Iva and filly

Iva and Marabona bathing filly

5

Lost in Translation

Tropical Park, Coral Gables, Florida December 1967

I got my trainer's license in March of 1964. From then until present, the A.W. Pollock stable had grossed twenty-five dollars from a fourth place finish at Sunshine Park. But finally, after three years of watching my horses finishing up the lane, I was about to saddle my first winner. His name was Nadecele, and by the luck of the draw, he was facing a field of 100-1 shots that couldn't beat their own shadow racing into the sun.

So I'm in the office, about to name Howie Grant on Nadecele, when I meet my friend Joe, who tells me that there is a special apprentice named Angel Cordero who was rumored to be "exceptional." If I rode Grant, I'd carry 126, but with Cordero I'd get a ten-pound apprentice break and only carry 116. Well, to me, weight in a short race is like "tits on a stud pig"—meaningless— but Joe kept insisting that it can't hurt to carry less weight, and since it didn't really matter who rode him, I put a line through H. Grant 126 and replaced it with A.E. Cordero 116.

Now I started counting the hours until racing history would he made—my first winner. As I walked Nadecele from the stable area to the paddock, I thought how Joe Louis must have felt walking from his dressing room before his second fight with Max Schmeling; it's all relative.

It all started to happen quickly now. The valet and I saddled Nadecele, and right after checking his girth strap for the fourth time, Angel Cordero approached with his hand extended and a big smile. I shook his hand and said that Nadecele needed to be loose reined in the gate.

"Just sit loose on him, and let him run into the bit. From there you'll just have to guide him."

Angel then looked up at me and said, "I give you good ride, boss!"

"See you in the winner's circle," I said as I threw him up.

"I give you good ride boss," he repeated as he rode off, and I proceeded to wallow in the moment.

I wondered how many winner's circle pictures I should order. Should I send one to my parents? "Three minutes to post time," the PA voice said, which was a signal to light a cigarette. "It is now post time," and like everyone else I stood up and leveled my binoculars at the starting gate just as the field got away.

I fully expected Nadecele to be in the first flight before he took the lead, but I couldn't find him anywhere. The field started to spread out now, but I still couldn't find him. I heard the announcer say " . . . and Nadecele trails." Nadecele trails? He was so far back he was in another area code. I couldn't believe my eyes; he could see them all!

In those days there was no such thing as instant replay; you just had to wait until the next day to see the film patrol in the steward's office which explained everything. It seems that Nadecele broke with his head down fighting the bit and thus pulling Angel almost between his ears, then, out of survival instinct . . . Angel pulled back on the reins, causing Nadecele to rear up like a wild stallion. By this time, of course, the field was out of sight.

I couldn't stop bitching. I would tell anyone who would listen, "All I told him to do was 'loose rein him in the gate,' and he didn't do it."

One of the recipients of my bitching was trainer Frank Martin who, in between giggles, said that Angel doesn't understand *any* English. His friends had taught him to say, "I give you good ride boss," when the American trainer's' instructions ended and his lips stopped moving.

A new way to lose, I thought.

P.S. Howie Grant was fluent in English.

And Warner Lipham said, "That's a real blivy."

Angel Cordero and I,
2009 Kentucky Derby

6

Listen My Children, And You Shall Hear of the Midnight Ride of Luke Greneer

Shenandoah Downs, Charleston, West Virginia, circa 1965

Shenandoah Downs is nestled in the beautiful Shenandoah Valley, in West Virginia. Not only is it picturesque, but it was also the first track to host night thoroughbred racing in America.

Since As night racing was in its infancy, it had its flaws. One of them was discovered by jockey Luther Greneer.

One foggy Saturday evening, Luke rode by my barn and discreetly said, "I'm gonna win the last race tonight."

"Who are you riding?" I asked. "Doesn't matter," he said, and rode off with a wink and a nod.

Now, I'm a believer in the old adage, "If you want to get rich, make book in the jockeys' room," but this was different; his remark, "it doesn't matter" really intrigued me. I sensed malfeasance in the air. Shenandoah Downs was a "bull ring" as half-mile tracks were referred to in those days, with a chute behind the top of the stretch enabling six furlong races to start up the chute passing the stands twice before the finish. According to custom, the last race Saturday night was a mile-and-half marathon. And Luke was riding Veranda, an eight-year-old mare that couldn't go a mile-and-a-half in a van. But judging from the expression on Luke's face, he could have been riding Man O'War.

You could barely make out the start because of the fog, but as the field went by the stands the first time, Veranda, was second on the outside under a good hold. But down the back stretch she started to drop back, and by the time they entered the stretch, I couldn't find her.

I combed the back stretch with my binoculars but I still couldn't see her. Cursing the fact that I actually listened to that pinhead, I headed for the exits, swearing that this was the last jockey's tip I'll ever play. Just before I reached my car, I heard the PA announcer say, "Caravan Queen still by a length on Extra Honey and Veranda coming fast on the outside."

I immediately did an about-face and ran back to the track in time to hear, "That's Veranda, and she owns the racetrack." What can I say? As I was cashing my ticket I was wondering who was the better jockey, Eddie Arcaro, Willie Schoemaker or Luther Greneer?

Sure enough, the next morning he comes to my barn strutting like a pacer, with coffee and donuts for all.

"I sure owe you one Luther," I said. "I didn't think she could go further than three quarters of a mile."

"She can't," Luther replied with a smile.

But before I could get him to explain himself, he bid me "Good day," and was gone. I never figured out what he did, but the stewards did. It seems that while watching the film patrol, they noticed that Veranda disappeared soon after the start and didn't re-appear until the stretch when she was drawing away from the field. It was alleged that Veranda was pulled up the first time she reached the back stretch and stood in the fog in the chute until the field had completed the first mile. At that point they simply sprinted down the stretch to win going away.

After listening to all of Luther's denials, head steward Ezra Beane suspended him for life in West Virginia.

Warner Lipham, after hearing the story said, "Damnedest job of rating I've ever heard."

I knew Veranda couldn't go beyond three-quarters of a mile!"

7

Eat at Joe's

Unlike Luther Greiner's unique shenanigans, the most common method of "taking your best shot" (as it used to be known) is with the battery, also known as "the joint "or help stick. It consisted of a flashlight-sized battery connected to a small device that, when pressed against a horses neck or flanks, makes him forget his age or any malady he may have for a while.

Needless to say, the stewards are aware of such behavior (lots of them are former jockeys) and do all they can to detect the signs. When a horse is "hit" during a race, his tail will shoot out straight while his speed is accelerated. An unnatural move by a jockey's hand is another thing the stewards look for.

So when Jay "Bucky" Turner won his fourth race of the day, the stewards were ready. State troopers met Jay in the winner's circle and escorted him back to the jockey's room where he was stripped and every inch of his clothing searched—all to no avail.

Now, it was time for the feature race and Jay (all the while proclaiming his innocence and threatening legal action) was escorted back to the paddock where his saddle, silks, whip and bridle were searched again before he was allowed to mount for the next race.

True to her custom, Alma L. (Jay's mount) trailed the field early, then approaching the far turn, Jay leaned forward, making several suspicious moves with his hands, which sent Alma L. bolting from last to first before the field reached the top of the stretch. It might as well have said "Eat at Joe's" on her neck. Now, with her tail as straight as a yard stick, Alma L. drew off, giving Jay his fifth win of the day.

State troopers, as well as the stewards were waiting for him in the winner's circle, "helped" him dismount, watched him weigh out, and shadowed him hack to the jockey's room, where he was again stripped and every article of apparel searched to no avail, even removing the heels of his boots. When detectives returned from searching the infield empty handed, a procession of bewildered law enforcement officers silently left the jockey's room.

It was about this time that Alma L. had been bathed, and was walking the shed with the joint securely tied in her bushy mane.

8

Watch Out, Jenny Craig

One of the difficulties of being a jockey is making the assigned weight; not the case at Sunshine Park in the early sixties. That is, not the case for Jesse Porter. Jesse was a five-foot-eight exercise rider with a jockey's license who rarely got a ride in the afternoon, but this afternoon he was riding Sandman, the heavy favorite in the last race.

Here's where Jenny Craig comes in. All jockeys are required to weigh in before the race. When Jesse stepped on the scale he miraculously went from 146 to 119 in the time it took to slip the clerk of scales a twenty dollar bill.

Now carrying more weight than Citation ever did Sandman and Jesse came home by five open lengths, paying $3.80 to win and sending almost everyone home happy. (Except the clerk of scales who backed his knowledge of the situation with a twenty dollar win bet on Nirisbi.)

And Warner Lipham said, "That's the way it goes; first your money, then your clothes."

9

Female Jockeys

Long before Mary Bacon, Barbara Jo Rubin or Julie Krone; even before Ruffian burned her bra, there was an event called The Powder Puff Preakness.

This was a non-betting exhibition race run on Preakness day between female exercise riders wearing "real" jockey silks, which would run the length of the stretch only. The sexist mentality of the times supported the idea that girls couldn't control horses going around turns (even though they did it every morning.) The safety factor was the cover story created to appease the mediocre male jockeys who refused to ride with female jockeys who would take some of their rides.

Sex in the Workplace

For the newly emerging female jockeys' agents, like Izzy Miranda (Mary Bacon's agent), the job description took on a whole new flavor. Pitches describing talents in the saddle held trainers' attentions like never before! It certainly wasn't lost on me and I told Izzy I would put Mary on Noonday Sun.

The next morning, I was waiting with my best winners circle smile when Mary, more gorgeous than I imagined, approached the barn. I had Noonday Sun saddled up and waiting for her, as well as clean sheets on the bed in the tack room. My expectations burst as soon as Mary took a look at Noonday Sun's ankles, which in the morning light resembled two ripe cantaloupes.

I said, "Hiya Mary," and without a response, she walked by me as if I were a parked car. "Is that a no?" I screamed to the trail of dust she left behind. A horse, a horse, my kingdom for a good horse!

Mary Bacon

10

They're Like Faded Photographs Now, But I Remember Woody Stephens

Hialeah Track Kitchen circa 1966 about 5:30 A.M

Woody would share his views on racing with anyone who would listen.

On career advancement: "Boys, if you wanna be a big flea, find yourself a big dawg." (He found Harry Guggenheim, Cain Hoy stables.)

About an hour later, riding my Appaloosa by his barn: "Anything to go to the track, Mr. Stephens?"

"You can have this rascal Al, don't lose him."

Still later that afternoon, giving instructions to jockey Johnny Rotz: "Ride 'em like you own 'em, John."

With his horse in front, turning for home you might hear: "Hang on to that rope!"

When his horse made a move from behind, he'd snap his fingers and yell, "Strike lightning.'"

On losing a close photo finish: "You win, you go home; you lose, you go home."

IVA MAE PARRISH -
Owner & trainer
Six furlongs
Time - 1:16:3

"Hasten Home"

PETER BRANDT up
Highly Dangerous- 2nd
Some Missile - third
Florida Downs, 2/22/67

Ditters holds Hasten Home,
25 January 1966

Ditters holds Hasten Home, 22 February 1967

REMAD

Frank Callico-up   6 furlongs   1:12.1 f
                20 September 1967   Detroit
A. H. Pollock, Owner and Trainer
Jealois, 2nd.   New Dack, 3rd.
              $16.20 $11.60 $7.00

Remad, 20 September 1967

" THE NATHAN JEWELERS "

"Nadecele"

1) PETER BRANDY up
Owner - Trainer
Florida Downs, Fla.
January 29, 1968

A. H. POLLOCK, owner
Lollipen - second
Star Romeo - third
Six furlongs 1:12¼

Nadecele, 29 January 1968

"The NEW FLORIDA HOTEL trophy"

Hasten Home

IVA MAE PARRISH,
Owner & trainer
5 1/2 furlongs
Time- 1:09 flat

PETER BRANCH up
Freedom Rider - 2nd
Ashby - third
Fla. Downs - 3/8/67

Everitt at head of Hasten Home, 8 March 1967

2nd Race in 2nd Half **Twin Double**

NINTH RACE

CLAIMING

PURSE $5,500. Four Year Olds and Upward. Non-winners of a Race Since February 1.

ONE MILE

MAKE SELECTION BY NUMBER

1 **TURKEY FOOT ROAD** 115

2 **DAVE'S PRIDE** 117

3 **B-8 GUN** 115

4 **BRONZINO** 110

5 **RED DARE** 115

6 **JAMBOREENA** 110

7 **SPRING BID** 115

8 **PRINCE GRAPHIC** 115

9 **STIPEND'S BOY** 115

10 **BUSH BEAU** 115

Selections: 1-3-2-6

NO MATTER WHERE YOU ARE — HAZEL PARK IS NEVER

Prince Graphic, No. 8, 1968, Hazel Park

11

Johnny Campo

Belmont Park circa 1969

Every boondocker dreams of someday running at the "races" (as the big time tracks were referred to). My one chance came in the fall of 1969. I had a filly that could compete, named Stuck Plenty, and incredibly she was the morning line favorite at 2-1.

The *Morning Telegraph* said, "fleet Michigan invader," but Johnny Campo's comment was somewhat different.

I drew the rail and Campo's filly, Mariners Joeie was number two. After saddling, Campo poked his head into my stall and said, "Hey Al, wadya gonna do with that mare? Milk her?"

Mariners Joeie won easily. Stuck Plenty came in fifth.

Maybe I should have milked her!"

12

Bill Christmas

Pimlico 1959

I'm having a Danish and coffee in the track kitchen after the races, and trainer Bill Christmas stops by my table and says:

"That's all you're having for dinner?"

I said, "I tapped out on Don Junior in the seventh."

He said, "You mean you bet your eatin' money?"

I said, "I wasn't hungry then." He bought me a fried chicken dinner.

13

Trainer Warner Lipham: Maxim Doo Da.

(A Man that makes Jeff Foxworthy seem
London born and raised.)

5 a.m., Stable Area Sunshine Park, Oldsmar, FL Winter 1963

Warner Lipham walked out of the darkness early one morning long, long ago and said in one syllable, "How are you this morning?"

Although stunned at witnessing this seemingly impossible feat, I managed to reply, "Still in the hunt Warner,"

"Good place to be, Yank," he said before once again disappearing into the morning darkness.

I was privileged to be stabled in the vicinity of this man for my eleven winters in Tampa in which time I regularly heard his opinion on:

Geography: *Home is where the money is.*
On Someone Who Practices Economy: *He's got short arms and deep pockets.*
On Religion: *Reckon that'll hep?*
Illustrating a Difficult Endeavor: *Can't git pups from a split bitch.*
To Emphasize Meaningless: *Like tits on a stud pig.*

Finance: *Can't go broke makin' money.*
On How Life Is Treating Him: *Good thing cows can't fly.*
On A Sudden Drop in Temperature: *Cold as Eskimo pussy.*
On Winning With a Favorite: *Better'n keeping him tied up.*
Responding To a Female's Smile: *Her tail's up now.*
On Someone Who Out Stays Their Welcome: *Like a turd that won't flush.*
On A Florida Rain: *Now we'll find out where the corn's planted.*
On Home Cooking: *Fulla Goodness*
Secret To Success: *Try and keep myself in the best company possible, and my horses in the worst.*

———

I remember the players as well, or better put ; how the everyday players made the money to come every day.

14 Al "The Brain" Gumper

Al was a bookmaker, as well as a better, and made a living at both. His biggest claim to fame was that he was busted twice in the same day but still made it to the track for the fifth race. It was one of the few times that he missed the daily double. In fact, he was there so often that the eighth pole said to the finish line, "He's here more than we are."

15

The Maitre'd
(Name Unknown)

He arrived at the track every day, dressed and groomed like a model. I don't remember seeing him in the same outfit twice. Of course all of this was understandable in his line of work.

He cruised the outdoor cafes looking for tourist types who were finishing their meal. As soon as the check was delivered and the server was out of sight, he would approach the table and inquire, "How was everything?" He would then pick up the folder with the check and the cash inside and head for the exits like a quarter horse in a stable fire.

I always marveled at the precision necessary to do this, since he only had a few seconds between the delivery of the check and the re-appearance of the server. I have often wondered how the emergence of credit cards has affected his career, because I haven't seen him at the track in a long time.

16

The Fixer
(Name withheld)

Most "Every day—ers" can he found exactly where you left them the day before, but not the Fixer. If he wasn't at the track, he was in court. It was well known that he had connections in high places and he maintained a lucrative legal career helping criminals stay out of jail when the outcome of their case could go either way.

His deal went something like this: He didn't take any money up front from his "clients." He would assure them that he would contact his political apparatus in their behalf and only accept compensation upon their release. Then if his client "walks," he would be waiting in the back of the courtroom with a big smile and his hand held out.

There's no telling how many friends and how much money this has made him over the years, because he would occasionally show up at the track with an entourage of shady hero worshippers. The amazing facet of this scenario, was that none of it was illegal because what he actually did was nothing—nothing whatsoever.

He knew no cops, no politicians or assistant D.A.'s—no one. He simply obtained the court dates of his clients, and if they "walked" he was there. If they left the court room with a uniformed escort however, well . . . the evidence was just too overwhelming against them. But they could be assured that he would explore all options for a successful appeal.

Warner Lipham, upon hearing the details, responded "That's as strong as homemade mustard."

17

The Count
(Nothing to do with royalty)

If there is a poker game, a crap game, a bunch of guys going to the track or even a bunch of guys going on a junket to Las Vegas, his response was the same: "Count me in."

18

Willie the Monarch

According to the History Channel, sometime in the spring of 1895, Kaiser Wilhelm of Germany visited his royal relatives in England. Every visit included an afternoon at Epsom Downs in the Queens royal box.

I had to wonder whether a monarch bets? If so, how much would make it interesting? How does he get down? Does the Queen Mother set him up with the family's Royal Bookmaker? Does his pointed helmet fall off while he's rooting? After having a winner, does he take the time to tell everyone in the royal party how he picked him? When he loses, does he accuse the races of being fixed?

Unofficial accounts of that particular afternoon reveal that Willie the Monarch lost every race and stormed out of the track bellowing, *"Dieses ist das letzte Mal, das dies unehrliche Pherden rennen mich sieht* ("this is the last time this crooked track is seeing me").

The next day, on the way back to Epsom Downs, he reassured his cousins that there would never be a revolution in England as long as there was horseracing. He must have seen that at the track, people shed their everyday masks and behave as if there is nothing else happening in the world.

So far he's been right. There's been horseracing in England since the twelfth century, and there hasn't been a revolution yet.

19

"Sometimes You Git Chickens ... Sometimes You Git Feathers"

Warner Lipham

Around 1960, Iva Mae Parrish bought a yearling by County Clare out of Miss Yuma for fifty cents named Hasten Home. Upon his retirement at age twelve, he had won thirty-nine races, with scores of seconds and thirds.

That's Chickens

February 2006, a British bookmaker named Michael Tabor bought a yearling by Forestry out of Magical masquerade for sixteen million dollars and named him Green Monkey. Upon his retirement at age four, he had accumulated possibly $6000 coming in third, fourth and fifth in three maiden races.

That's Feathers

20

Miscellaneous Memories

Tampa, Miami or Detroit

Every morning, Efrain "Frank" Garcia would emerge from his Cadillac before dawn dressed like a migrant farm worker, then disappear after training hours, only to reappear in the clubhouse that afternoon looking like he just left a barber shop in a custom-made silk suit.

Monmouth Park

In 1957, the leading jockey at Monmouth Park was a man named Sammy Boulmetis. One day he was on a very heavy favorite that couldn't possibly lose. When he did, a voice behind me bellowed loud enough that Aristotle could hear him, "Nice race Boulmetis, ya Greek bastard."

I had to wonder, "did this man hate Greeks before the race? I'm sure it never entered his mind. Going home it was probably a different story. If Eddie Arcaro, Walter Blum, George Grabowski, Angel Valenzuela or Conn McCreary had ridden that horse, the expletive would have been different. The reason this event stands out in my memory is that it was, in fact, the only racial slur I ever heard at the racetrack.

Tampa

I went to the track doctor in Tampa feeling like mildewed garlic. When I reassured him that I react well to penicillin, he said, "Son, penicillin won't hep, you got the creepin' virus. You just gotta wait for it to creep on out." And he was right . . . it crept on out.

During a poker game, Ed Harmon drew a three of spades to a heart flush. With restrained anger, he looked up at the ceiling and said, "Thank ya, thank ya kindly."

One morning in Tampa when Johnny Roan's name came up, Iva Mac stopped what she was doing and said, "He squeezes a nickel so tight, could make the buffalo holler."

Upon hearing a quarreling couple in the grandstand, Travis Booth, without looking up from his *Racing Form*, said "there's no poontang in his immediate future."

When I won a three horse photo finish with Stuck Plenty I was basking in my elation when Warner Lipham approached me and said, "Hey, Yank, how'd it feel when they put your number up?"
I'll tell you exactly how it felt, Warner. It felt like when a woman says "yes."
"I can appreciate that," Warner responded.

Detroit

Most every morning in Detroit as soon as he wasn't alone, Willie the Groom would say, "Hey, lookee here "as he gyrated like Elvis Presley, pointing to his groin, "got me some hump loving last night"

On a typical Detroit morning at Ernie's Diner, while selecting a donut, I bump into Jamaican Sam. "Howya doin' Sam?" I said.

"Oh jus' drinkin', gamblin', cryin' and smokin' the herb mon."

Hialeah

The track announcer said, "That's Cool Jack, delaying the start."

To which Travis Booth put down his binoculars and said, "At least I got a call."

New York, Detroit, Tampa or Miami

At some point in any poker game, Al Pollock is sure to say, "I've seen better hands in arthritis wards."

21

Memories Of Detroit

"You all Yankees goin' up yonder to Dee-troit?" Warner Lipham asked when he saw me packing up my tack, binoculars, and stop watch. Detroit was my summer place throughout the turbulent 60s . . . a time when it was impossible not to hear Diana Ross or the Jackson Five on your radio, even if it wasn't turned on. There seemed to be boundless prosperity. The auto plants worked three eight hour shifts a day, brilliantly staggered to completely avoid a rush hour.

It appeared as though everyone drove a new Chevy or Ford. The rich people drove Cadillacs, and I don't remember ever seeing a foreign car. It was bizarre that within this atmosphere of prosperity, the Michigan National Guard, backed up by tanks, were putting down riots on Woodward Avenue. Downtown Detroit looked like the Battle of Berlin. The only reason I knew about the riots at all was that I saw them on television. Hazel Park was a good five miles from the chaos and life there went on as usual as if this was happening in Vietnam. This is not to say we were completely oblivious to the possible ramifications of the disturbances. As a matter of fact, there was a running debate in the track kitchen about whether any of this would affect the horses.

22

The Science Of
Thoroughbred Training

Hazel Park, Detroit 1968

Long, long ago, when I was less refined, I owned a horse named
Prince Graphic, whose only positive attributes were that he was
a superior mud runner and he liked carrots. He was nine years
old and cranky, but if he caught a sloppy track and there was
no other front runner (speed horse) in the race, he actually had
a chance to win. Otherwise he usually did the moonwalk in the
stretch. Occasionally, running in a small field, he got fourth. (I
think I spent that whole summer rooting for him to get fourth.)

It's never easy to get out of bed at 4:30 am. But on the morning
of July 11, when my clock radio blasted "I Heard It Through
the Grapevine," it was not the song, but rather the familiar splat
of Detroit rain that was music to my ears. Prince Graphic was
running today, and I couldn't wait to grab a *Racing Form* and
check out the field.

Willie the Groom and Prince Graphic 7/68

The first six horses were stretch runners and then there was Flip By, the fly in the ointment. He was the worst kind of horse to be in there with because he always went out for the lead. The fact that he also always finished last, however, gave me an idea.

Later that morning, I went looking for Noah Wayne, Flip By's regular jockey. I spotted him in the track kitchen. He was reading the *Racing Form* as I approached him with a coffee in either hand. We talked about today's races and finally got to the ninth, where we were both entered.

That's when I said, as if it had just occurred to me, "Did you ever think of changing tactics with Flip By?"

He said, "We've tried everything but he just won't rate."

I replied, "Well, since you're going to come last anyway, why don't you just stand up on him at the start as if he stumbled and pull him over to the rail. He won't run up heels, right? Then, when you're clear you can go for it. Just give me the first half mile."

At that point it occurred to Noah, "That'd leave you alone on the lead, wouldn't it?"

And I replied, "But that'd leave you with fifty bucks you didn't have before." Noah had gotten the drift. He took the fifty and assured me with his eyes that he would do what was expected.

In the paddock, I told jockey Gaddis to hustle Prince Graphic to the lead and kick mud back in their faces. He said, "What about Flip By? He'll burn us out."

I told him, "Just shoot ducks and see what happens. He's got his track today." When the bugle blew, I threw him up and simply said "Hurry back," and headed to the windows.

I bet him across the board, lit a cigarette, and watched the Prince warm up on his favorite track. He looked like he was having so much fun that I went back and bet him again, knowing that he'd never have a better setup than this.

Everyone did their parts; Gaddis rushed Prince Graphic out of the gate and Noah, on Flip By, stood up at the start and pulled him behind the field on the rail. Prince Graphic had it his way. He was the only horse in my binoculars (either lens.)

Around the far turn we had a five-length lead over a once strung out field. It was looking good until several large animals showed up in my right lens. When the field straightened out it was clear he was going to get caught. No sooner had I resigned myself to second than I see my Prince looking for a comfortable place to lie down. All right, I'll take third. Just as I conceded that, a muddy blur shot up on the outside, nipping me on the wire for third money. Wanna guess who it was? It was Noah Wayne on Flip By. And now things got even better. Willie the Groom didn't show up to take the Prince of Fourth Money back to the barn, leaving me the pleasure of walking him hack in the pouring rain. As I headed toward the barn, Noah Wayne walked by and said, "Hey, Al, you showed me how to ride this horse."

About three weeks later, after Flip By's second come-from-behind victory in a row, his trainer, Eli Gander, was interviewed by Joe Falls of the *Detroit Free Press* in a human interest column. Joe asked him how he turned his horse around from coming last all the time to a third and two wins in his last three starts. "I'm a horseman, Joe' he replied somewhat arrogantly, "a good trainer develops a communication with his horse. You learn to listen to what your horse is telling you and Flip By was telling me he needed a change in tactics."

That winter, when I told Warner Lipham this story he said, "Eli Gander . . . ain't no one in all creation who knows exactly how dumb this man really is."

23

They

Webster defines "they" as a third person pronoun referring to a group or several but at the racetrack "they" implies the invisible power that controls every outcome; "they knew," "they won't let a favorite win the last race," "they know the jockey," and the one that's lasted a millennium—"they always let you win at first."

On September 20th, 1967 for ten minutes, I was they.

About three weeks before that day, I was at Finger Lakes Racetrack in upper New York State getting ready to ship to Tampa for the winter. Along with Prince Graphic and Alfred (my Appaloosa) I had a pretty good five thousand dollar claimer who was just a few weeks from a race. He had developed ankle problems over the summer and I wasn't taking any chances with him by starting him too soon or as Warner Lipham, that scholar of Southern culture and verse would say, "If ya don't wait, they'll make you wait."

The next morning fate intervened. I was visited by the racing secretary who said nicely but firmly that they needed a horse to fill a race and since I started only one horse all summer, he thought of me. I told him that Remad was a race short and that I was going to run him that way. That seemed to be okay and not anxious to press the issue, he simply said "Just fillin' heats, Al" and walked away.

In the paddock, I told the jockey, Richard Marsh, why he was entered and instructed him to let him rattle on his own until he backs up . . . then just let him go without abusing him . . . and this should set him up for next time.

Well, they'll make a liar out of you every time. Remad broke with the pack and stayed in the hunt for a good half mile. Then, when I thought he would back up , he seemed to find another gear and made a run at the leaders. Just when I thought he was sure for second or third, the nightmare happened: he bobbled right before my eyes and was immediately eased, visibly lame. As I walked my now-crippled horse back to the barn, I could only visualize Remad rearing up and bringing down his crippled leg on the racing secretary's head. When I got to the barn, I bathed Remad and began to walk him around the shed. I could feel his soreness with every stride he took until suddenly his gait changed and he was walking sound. Afraid it might be temporary, I held my breath until the next morning, knowing that if his ankle was cold then, he was sound. If it was feverish, it would be months before he would race again.

I arrived at the barn at 5 a.m., only to see that my friend Joe had beaten me there. He greeted me with a big smile and said, "That ankle's as cold as a well-digger's ass."

I, of course, had to see for myself and as soon as I felt those cold ankles against my cheek, I knew he was okay. As the sun rose that morning, people stopped by the barn to offer their condolences based on yesterday's events, and I happily shared my good news with everyone. What an idiot! Now I had a horse worth every bit of five grand, perfectly sound and fit to win, and had I not opened my big mouth, I could have put him in at the bottom right here at Finger Lakes next week and gotten 20 to 1 for my money.

But now full exploitation of the situation required a change of venue. Well, the choices were to run Remad at the bottom at either Aqueduct, Detroit Race Course, Garden State or Windsor in Canada. Canada was too complicated, Aqueduct or Garden State he could win or he could lose, but in Detroit he was as sure as horseshit in Kentucky. I mean he could win with a howitzer tied to his tail.

On the morning of the race, I waited anxiously for the morning papers to see how we were picked (or not picked.) The *Racing Form's* comment was, "returned lame in last."

The *Detroit Free Press* said, " Remad . . . make you mad."

The *Detroit News* simply picked him last saying, "dull New York invader." He was 30 to 1 in the program but he should have been 1 to 5 ! How do you describe the feeling of saddling a 1 to 5 shot that is currently 99 to 1 on the board.

I guess it was the way Willie Sutton must have felt just before the safe opened. I could barely keep my hands from shaking as I entered the paddock and instructed jockey Frank Callico to "ride him like you own him." I told him not to worry, "he's as sound as a bell of brass."

Well, I bet my money (all but ten dollars just in case he jumped the fence,) and proceeded to light a cigarette and wondered how I was going to feel a few minutes from now.

The man said, "It is now post time." I raised my binoculars but closed my eyes. I couldn't take the anxiety, knowing what was at stake. When I opened my eyes Remad was five lengths in front and improving his position. The rest of the field was so far behind they could have been running the next race.

As Remad crossed the finished line eased up, I couldn't help but notice that the 99 on the board was now a 7. As shocking as that was, I still made it to the winner's circle in time to pose for the picture, wondering all the while where Mary Bacon would be riding this winter.

My big moment, however, was yet to come. As I was headed to the window to cash in, I overheard a voice say, "They sneaked him in from Finger Lakes." For a brief moment, I stood beside Hirsch Jacobs, Sunny Jim Fitzsimmons and Woody Stephens, but as soon as the bugle blew for the second race, people turned the pages of their programs and it was over. It is unlikely that I will ever be elected to the Racing Hall of Fame, but I'll always have those moments when I was "they."

And Warner Lipham said, "You're still just another Yank to me."

24

A Fantasy Is The Hardest Thing to Give Up

As Upset was the most aptly named horse of all time, Up the Lane Jane has to be second. She possessed a fierce resistance to any speed whatsoever; in fact her fastest move was from her water bucket to her feed tub. In short, she was the opposite of Zenyetta. She was the only horse I ever trained that I didn't own (thank God). This distinction belonged to Mr. Andrew Burns from Dearborn. Andy would show up most mornings before dawn, seeking a report on Jane's progress. Did she eat up? Move her bowels? Swat flies? He'd inquire about my planned regimen for Jane's training program and tell me, "I don't want to see any black type in the papers."

For those of you who have never owned a racehorse, inaccurate perceptions are the rule rather than the exception An owner tends to identify with his horse, and the horse's victories and losses become his own. In other words, he becomes his horse. That said, how do I tell Andy that Jane walks and gallops at the same speed? How do I tell him that the closest she ever got to the field was in the paddock and that the only way he'll ever cash a ticket on her will be if she is scratched at the gate?

I was always amazed how shocked and disappointed Andy would continue to be after each devastating defeat (once by the entire length of the stretch.) Finally I said to him, "Andy, you have here a beautiful animal that is 100 percent sound, who's telling us in her way that she wants a career change." I then suggested the Michigan show circuit. This appeased his ego enough for him to agree. On the day they left, I wished him luck.

"Luck has nothing to do with this," he turned to me and said with a wink and a smile. "I see nothing but blue ribbons in our future."

———

Speaking of fantasies, I had some of my own (not all involving Mary Bacon.)

One morning, while driving to Hazel Park, I heard Diana Ross singing, "Can't Hurry Love" on the radio. Between the hosiery shops, the donut shops and the record stores that bore her name, Diana Ross was everywhere. That's when I had the brainstorm. I bet Diana Ross would love to own racehorses! I could see a barn full of expensive horses named Reflections, Baby Love, The Happening, etc. I even imagined Baby Love's name on the 1969 Kentucky Derby Julep glass. I would, of course, be her trainer.

It's amazing how quickly a fantasy becomes reality if you want it badly enough. By the time I got to the track, I had her silks picked out, her stable name and a half dozen names for her horses. Now, how do I get to speak to her?

At first I thought I'd try to reach her at home, where there'd be fewer distractions. That turned out to be a bust because no one, including the operator, seemed to know where she lived. My only other option was Motown Records.

"Motown Records, Good afternoon."

"Hi, Diana Ross please."

Pause. "Who should I say is calling?"

"Al Pollock."

Pause again. "From where, Mr. Pollock?"

"Hazel Park."

"You mean the racetrack?"

"Yes."

"One moment please."

New Voice: "Hello, Miss Ross isn't here. Is she expecting your call?"

"Not exactly, but I only need about ten minutes of her time."

"One moment please." Pause.

Third Voice: "Hello, sir, Miss Ross isn't here right now, but if you leave your phone number, I'll make sure that she gets it."

"Oh, okay, I'll hold on."

"No, no, she won't be here anymore today. She has a show at the Ford Theatre this evening. Don't worry, if you leave your number, I will personally see that she gets it."

That sounded reasonable, so I left the number of the phone booth outside of my barn. To my disappointment, she still hadn't called by the next morning. Well, I thought, last night was opening night, she must have been busy. If I don't hear from her soon, I'll just go down to the Ford Theatre tonight and catch her before her next show.

I arrived at the theater at 5 o'clock and waited. About 6:15, something that resembled the presidential motorcade pulled up to the stage door. I thought, should I wait in my car until everyone got settled? It wasn't until 7 o'clock that I knocked on the stage door.

"May I help you?"

"Yes, I'd like to see Diana Ross for a few minutes."

"She didn't say she was expecting anyone, and she's really not available at the moment"

"Oh, I understand. I'll Wait. The show doesn't start for about two hours so we've got plenty of time."

"Why don't you leave your phone number and I'll see that she gets it."

Now I'm getting annoyed. "I already did that and she didn't call me back! Why do you think I'm here?"

"Just a moment, I think I see her."

"It's about time."

He shut the stage door, and after a few minutes it re-opened revealing two guys that could have been rejected by the Detroit Lions for being so big that they could seriously hurt someone.

Before they could say anything, I told them, "I've been waiting here since five o'clock to see Diana Ross. It'll only take a few minutes."

Before I could say another word, the bigger one of the two bent down and placed his nose in front of mine and said, "Take a hike Frosty."

Back in my car, by the time I reached Woodward, I had accepted the fact that the Diana Ross thing was probably never going to happen. I lit a cigarette at a red light and flicked on the radio, "R-E-S-P-E-C-T." Yeah, I thought , that'll fit perfect on a derby glass. I'll call Aretha Franklin in the morning.

25

Then and Now

In my day, that is when horses ran on hay, oats and water, they were able to convey accurately to their trainers their ailments as well as their readiness to run. Now, with the prevalent use of legal drugs, a horse's real condition is not apparent until he goes lame caused by lack of treatment for his masked maladies.

That, in my opinion, is the biggest of the many changes that have occurred in the last fifty years. Two things, however, will never change: the beauty of the sun illuminating the stable area at dawn, and those two magical words that have carried us through the hardest of times: Tomorrow's Entries.

26

My Old Kentucky Home Good Night.

—and good night Mary Bacon, wherever you are.

Doo Da Dictionary

Eddie Arcaro:	Maybe the best jockey ever
Axe handles:	The scale of measurement of the female ass.
Bell of Brass:	As sound as a brass bell
Black type:	When a horse trains exceptionally fast, his name and workout are listed in darker type than the others.
Blivy:	Six pounds of manure in a five pound bag
Bottom:	Against worse horses on the grounds . . . cheapest race.
Bupkis:	Jewish term for "a little more than nothing"
Angel Cordero Jr.:	The best jockey ever
Currier and Ives:	Famous nineteenth-century artists that specialized in winter scenes.

Detroit Lions:	Local NFL team.
Doo Dah:	To Stephen Foster, it was an expression of jubilation. To me, it's the memory of a time when every day was Derby Day.
"Sunny" Jim Fitzsimmons:	Hall of Fame trainer
Gittin' chesty:	As in sticking one's chest out . . . . becoming more confident.
Hazel Park:	One of Detroit's two racetracks
Heats:	Nineteenth century term for races as in a "dead heat," referring to the fact that all bets are off . . . a tie.
Hep:	Help
In the hunt:	Close up in a race
Hirsh Jacobs:	Hall of Fame trainer
Moonwalk:	Walking backwards . . . from dance made famous by Michael Jackson
Pacer:	A standard bred with a stride that resembles a strut.
Pinhead:	What Iva Mae called jockeys
Poontang:	Vagina

Pumpernicks:	A large deli located a short walk from the stable area at Gulfstream, world-renowned for their early bird special.
Racing Secretary:	Man responsible for filling races.
Rank and Common:	When a horse fights his jockey's instructions.
Rating:	Conserving your speed early. Opposite of "shooting ducks"
Rikers Island:	New York City Prison
Ruffian:	Champion filly who broke down in match race with Kentucky Derby winner and had to be euthanized. It's not all doo da.
Rugelah:	Jewish pastry to die for
Willie Shoemaker:	Maybe the best jockey ever.
Shooting Ducks:	Going all out at the start. Opposite of rating.
Starting Short:	Using a race for workout purposes rather than winning.
Woody Stephens:	Hall of Fame trainer.
Squeegee rolls:	Any breakfast food that isn't grits
Stewards:	Overall authority at track.

Willie Sutton:	Famous bank robber
Tack:	Riding equipment . . . saddles, bridles, etc
Tack room:	Where tack is stored. Also used for poker games and safe sex
Tapped out:	The financial state of having less than one. In some states referred to as "tapioca."
Upset:	The only horse to beat Man O'War.
Up the Lane:	Finishing far behind the second to last horse.
Well digger's ass:	Body part deepest in the ground
Woodward Avenue:	Main thoroughfare in downtown Detroit.
Yank:	Nothing to do with baseball. Southern reference to anyone not Southern. Opposite of rebel.
Zenyetta:	Champion race mare.

www.ingramcontent.com/pod-product-compliance
Lightning Source LLC
Chambersburg PA
CBHW051636050426
42443CB00024B/292